THE BATTLE OF ONE OF GOD'S MANY SOLDIERS

GET BACK SATAN NOW

THE BATTLE OF ONE OF GOD'S MANY SOLDIERS

BTP Publishing

Unless otherwise indicated, all Scripture quotations in this volume are from the King James Version (KJV), New King James Version (NKJV), New International Version (NIV) and the English Standard Version (ESV) of the Bible.

Copyright © 2023 by Cody M. Arbuckle

All rights reserved. No part of this book may be reproduced in any manner whatsoever without written permission except in the case of brief quotations embodied in critical articles and reviews.

BTP Publishing, 2023

*The Battle of one of God's many soldiers.
The falling of the mask comes with
seeking one face.*

Read Carefully and Study!

You must first recognize the problem before you can see the solution!

PLAN OF ACTION

- Willingness to see the problem
- Make a decision to change the problem
- Belief in the most high to fix the problem

> L is for Living
> O is for Out
> V is for Victory
> E is for Everyday

Living Out Victory Everyday is the defeat of all evil!

GET BACK SATAN NOW

As I step out on faith I would like everyone who's taking the time out to read this, to know that life is in the power of the tongue!
I have faced many battles, but I come to realize the battle of many masks...

Listen to me clearly as I explain my journey. As I walk to seek one face. The face of the most high.

Forgiveness + Trust + Respect = Peace

Positive energy will always change everything

THE BATTLE OF ONE OF GOD'S MANY SOLDIERS

Ephesians 5:1 ESV
Therefore be imitators of God, as beloved children

Ephesians 4:1 NIV
As a prisoner for the Lord, then, I urge you to live a life worthy of the calling you have received

Proverbs 3:5-6 NIV
Trust in the Lord with all your heart, and lean not on your own understanding; in all your ways submit to him, and he will make your paths straight.

As we know the story of Noah,

> Genesis 9:21 New International Version
> When he drank some of its wine, he became
> drunk and lay uncovered inside his tent.

Now, I come to realize why ALCOHOLICS ANONYMOUS is the second riches book and the Bible is the first.

For a long time I thought I could pick up one drink and stop. I even tried to switch up my ways, but it all led to one thing...

Getting drunk again and doing drugs again. My choice of drug was cocaine. I once died for 15 minutes because fentanyl was in the cocaine which led me to quit for approximately six months. I then decided to leave my hometown to avoid my wicked ways and wrongdoing. Before you knew it, I was back to my old ways.

I tried quitting so many times, but I was hitting and missing while still trying to do the work of God. Until one day I had enough!

The enemy deceived me into believing that if I committed suicide all of my pain would be at a halt. I felt like a complete hypocrite. I checked myself into an AA program to remove myself from my contaminated environment to hear God's voice and to seek more help. I came to realize that yes, I have a disease. I was honest and upfront with myself. Yes, I am an addict and I have a mental obsession! I then knew the only way I could quit is to not pick up the very addiction that had me bound.

I've always been very big on love, but it was clear that I've been uneducated on the real meaning of love. Choosing my addiction over myself wasn't love at all. All the selfish self-centered ways, disobedience, alcohol and drugs is what lead me directly to AA. The program was very beneficial for me because the power of God and his everlasting love was evident.

A TRUE FACT

A Mental Illness can be a hand-full of things. Addiction is one.

Galatians 5:19-21 New International Version
[19] The acts of the flesh are obvious: sexual immorality, impurity and debauchery; [20] Idolatry and witchcraft; hatred, discord, jealousy, fits of rage, selfish ambition, dissensions, factions [21] and envy; drunkenness, orgies, and the like. I warn you, as I did before, that those who live like this will not inherit the kingdom of God.

God is amazing! He can heal you from addiction, iniquity, pain and suffering. To overcome it is important to recognize your bad habits and submit to what this outstanding verse is telling you. Make sure you meditate frequently. As much as you can, daily!

Lean on God's word and he will rescue and deliver you.

GET BACK SATAN NOW

2 Chronicles 7:14-18 New International Version
[14] if my people, who are called by my name, will humble themselves and pray and seek my face and turn from their wicked ways, then I will hear from heaven, and I will forgive their sin and will heal their land. [15] Now my eyes will be open and my ears attentive to the prayers offered in this place. [16] I have chosen and consecrated this temple so that my Name may be there forever. My eyes and heart will always be there.

[17] "As for you, if you walk before me faithfully as David your father did, and do all I command, and observe my decrees and laws, [18] I will establish your royal throne, as I covenanted with David your father when I said, 'You shall never fail to have a successor to rule over Israel.'

Recently I felt empty and alone. I believed that I was strong enough to overcome the pain I felt, but God revealed to me that my true strength comes from him and that is something I will never forget.

By the grace of God, I am still alive running the race of sobriety. I've learned to lean not on my own understanding and to constantly seek God's face.

God spoke to me during my time in AA. He instructed me to write a personal inventory of my life, on what I decided to let go and what I need to continue in order to remain clean and in his will. I realized that I held on to bad habits and selfish ways. Deep down I knew I had to fully surrender. I heard God's voice very clear, "The Battle of one of

THE BATTLE OF ONE OF GOD'S MANY SOLDIERS

God's many soldiers."I then decided to step out on faith and walk into the direction he called me towards.

When God is calling you to an assignment he will send people in your path to encourage you and uplift you to keep going! During AA I met a man of God whom was a deacon some time ago. His name was Travis. There were six people assigned to each room. Three on one side and three on the other. By God's grace it was just one person on my side of the room whom was Travis. As I sat on my bed he would come by and say, "Don't hold that word! What are you reading now?" In the room I was the only one who kept a bible on my side. I proceeded to tell him that I was in the middle of writing a book and I would also read my writings to him from time to time. Everyday I read the Bible and I prayed that God would bless me with more words because I only made it to page two for this very book he instructed me to write. Travis would uplift me, encourage me, he would also share with me his testimonies and the lessons he learned. He kept me in line when I got out of order because being in any captivity can be extremely hard mentally. A week in AA felt like an entire year! Although we were in captivity, there was a TV room, a yard for us, a laundry room, an eating area, a medical room, an educational room and a room full of beds for twenty males and twenty females to lay their head. My favorite area was the room where we all lay our heads. Alongside my bed was where I spent my intimate time with God, its where he instructed me to began writing. Around 6:30 a.m. we all would get up and head to the TV room to pray and give thanks. After we ate, we cleaned up together to show appreciation to each and everyone who lived and worked in the facility.

On the weekend we were allowed to have TV night. We all got together to choose a movie to watch out of three picks. I was the guy with all the snacks in my locker and everyone knew where to come to get what they needed. I was not allowed to have them... how I got them is another story!

I'll never forget the moment when we returned to our beds, I immediately dropped to my knees to pray. When I stood up I seen Travis and our new roommate on their knees praying also. I laid down and I thanked Jesus because that was the evidence of how powerful God can be through us as vessels. In AA we had group meetings four times daily. In our meetings we learned to listen and to care about others that were suffering from drug and alcohol addiction. One day during group, a young man stood up and said he wanted to have a clear understanding of God like me and the others. I was completely shocked and blessed at the same time. I had no knowledge of his story before leading up to AA, but I will never forget mine and that very moment reminded me of it. I've always been a happy person with a smile on my face, but I will never forget the moment when I completely lost it. I was heartbroken and I felt very alone before I entered AA. Church played a part in my restoration but I would still run back to drugs and alcohol. Entering AA completely changed my life. To be around people who were sober for decades and who was not afraid to talk about their story truly helped me.

After dealing with mental delusion I gained my sanity back. I was more than excited to speak with my wife, my mother and my mother in law again. After all I brought upon myself I found peace in knowing I still had love and family. The total required days to spend in AA was twenty eight and I was on day eleven. I noticed that others began to act strange towards me and wrongly accuse me of things because I would always quote scriptures. One day during group I decided to rebuke the devil. I told everyone that it is not okay for us all to turn against one another. I then left to go to my room to write a little and read the Bible.

Approximately a hour later I was called to the office to be questioned.

By day fourteen I was completely fed up and I made up in my mind that I was ready to return home. By eight o'clock in the morning during our AA group I stood up and I told everyone that I no longer desired to be in AA and I could no longer take how I was being treated. I grabbed all of my personal belongings and I went to the front of the facility to sign out of the program. A woman by the name of Ms. Tori worked in the front office and she was very understanding of my situation. I asked her if she believed that I could make it and stick to the plan of staying on track. She replied, "Yes baby, I am one hundred percent sure that you will. God will guide you." I truly needed those words.

A few moments later, the doctor walked in. She tried her best to convince me to stay but my decision was final. She walked me outside and we said our goodbyes. It was now time to get back to work and focus on becoming more like Christ. A few weeks had gone by and I finally finished the book God instructed me to write. I typed everything I had written and I proceeded to print sixteen copies. I passed ten of those copies out and it was back to the library to print more. My intentions were to print twenty more copies, but when I made it to my car after printing the twenty copies I realized that I had enough money to print three more copies. I walked back into the library and as I printed the last copy a very nice young lady walked up to me and said, "Hello sir, are you writing a book?" I replied, yes. She then proceeded to say, "I am a publisher and God told me to help you with your book."

Proverbs 3:6 ESV
In all your ways acknowledge him, and he will make straight your paths.

GET BACK SATAN NOW

Living Out Victory Everyday is the defeat of all evil! I want to Thank God for my Wife, Mr. Richard and Ms. Linda, My Mother, My Mother in Law, Tyrone, Pops, Mr. Robert, My Dad, Pastor John and his church, Mother Cyprian, Pastor Bickham of Evangelical Church of God in Christ, Pastor Lester and his church, Deacon Chris, My brother Fatback, Kristen Kilbey, Shontell Buffingtotn, DR.Pittman, Breana the Publisher, and many more! Thank you all.

Here are a few short stories and testimonies of those who have practiced Living Out Victory Everyday.

THE BATTLE OF ONE OF GOD'S MANY SOLDIERS

Dear God,
Whoever reads this, let it be a blessing to their soul...

I was asked to write about a situation God turned around in my life and as I write the word "born again" comes to mind. I know the Bible tells us to live by the power of our testimony, especially when hardships come (so we can endure the hardships as good soldiers 2 Timothy 2:1) and I've been through some hardships and I'm sure you have too. Some of mine consist of health and healing, death and life and the lost of freedom. I firmly believe that Jesus and thee shedding of his blood on Calvary to adopt us as it states in Ephesians 1:4-5. To know what I was is no longer who I am is all he ever wanted which is to be complete and whole in Christ Jesus. (Colossians 2:10) and to be a witness for his name sake and make his name great.

In Ephesians it states, "For he chose us in him before the creation of the world to be holy and blameless in his sight. In love he predestined us to be adopted as his sons through Jesus Christ, in accordance with his pleasure and will."

And right there is LOVE! Living Out Victory Everyday (John 3:16). No longer do I have to worry about I, but I choose to put him first and trust and cast all cares on him daily. I get a chance to renew my mind, renew my spirt and soul...something I can't do alone but only with him for he died for it all! The good, the bad and the ugly with no judgement but repentance. I don't know about you but that makes my soul grateful. I hope this message as well as this book blesses you as it has blessed me (Romans 10:9).

                                     Love, Jasmine Arbuckle

GET BACK SATAN NOW

Mrs. Powell, My Mother

For over 50 years I was torn and unhappy, no matter what I did, even going to my meeting, (Kingdom Hall) but for some reason I didn't understand why I never felt joy, even though I had so much love for God. I prayed and asked God to help me to get in there and feel something because I was always unhappy when I left. I went home and a friend of mine called me and she knew I was so unhappy. Little did I know that she had been in the same religion. She gave me some literature to read, but I was so scared to read it because I was in fear. All of my life I was taught not to read other literature or to never allow anyone to pray for me that was outside of my religion. I decided to read it anyway. After reading it I felt a certain kind of way. I still was fearful, but I wanted to know more because I remembered that I gave over 50 years to this religion I was in. I went to God and I prayed, I said "God I need you. I don't know exactly I'm asking for, but I trust you. Please guide me God." It took one prayer and after that prayer everything came to me. God really heard me and I believed that's what I prayed to God all those years. To help me feel some kind of way. When I was in that religion he didn't answer it because he had another plan for me. He knew that wasn't where I was supposed to be. Now I have joy after that prayer to God that you are my father in Jesus name
Amen

THE BATTLE OF ONE OF GOD'S MANY SOLDIERS

Pastor Lester

I was riding my motorcycle most of the day, and I decided to head back to the house. I had work on this particular day, so I needed to get ready for the evening. The Lord Jesus is my passenger as I talk with him and sing to him on my way home. The day was beautiful, exhilarating, and my heart was full of joy. I looked at the Main Street as I began riding through it to get home. Suddenly, there was a car sideways in my path! I grabbed the clutch, the front brake, and stomped the back brake, but the car-bike impact was instantaneous! I felt myself flying through the air while doing a complete flip and Jesus name came out my mouth in that split moment. So did the thought in my mind "This ain't going to be good!" In the next couple of seconds, I landed squatting in the road on the other side of the car with my hands on the pavement and the sole of my boots in the road and I sprained my thumb. Suddenly, while trying to figure out if I have gone to Heaven or if I'm still on Earth. I heard a young girls voice, hollering at me. "Mister! Mister! Did you see what you did? You turned a complete flip over the top of that car!" The little girl was completely full of joy over my evil knievel impression. As her mother grabbed her up, I was standing up! I began to thank Jesus as fast as I could! It is such moments as these that the reality of Jesus presence is the most desired presence of anyone. He was there to catch me in my time of need! His presence was the strength of my salvation and joy!

Adversity breeds character. I would not be who I am today had I not experienced adversity. There was a time in my life when I focused on everything that went wrong in my life. I focused on all the things that I didn't have. I focused on all of the people who let me down. I focused on all of the people who didn't stay. It was not until I was able to be thankful for those who God placed in my life to stand in the gap that I was able to praise God and know that everything that happened in my life was preparing me to be me. The me who God created me to be.

S.D. Buffington

My name is Kristen Kilbey. I grew up in a very violent, drug, and alcoholic family. I began to drink alcohol when I was thirteen. I began to do cocaine when I was fifteen. I did cocaine for 38 years. The three years of my addiction was crystal meth. I never put a needle in my arm. I had five violent boyfriends, all abusive drug related relationships. I got my third DUI, I was under the influence of crystal meth. That was the moment when I said that I had enough. I asked Jesus Christ to change my life. I repented for my sins and asked for forgiveness. I knew that I was done living that way. All we have to do is ask Jesus Christ into our hearts and repent, and turn away from our sins.

Jesus is coming soon, turn to him while he is still calling you.

THE BATTLE OF ONE OF GOD'S MANY SOLDIERS

Proverbs 13:13 New King James Version

He who despises the word will be destroyed, but he who fears the commandment will be rewarded.

Everything worth having isn't easy to obtain.
Jesus was called higher to save humanity and the devil tempted him every which way he could.

It is very important to stay sober and alert!
The devil comes to steal, kill, and destroy.
Don't give the enemy an open door to destroy you.

1 Peter 5:8-9 ESV

⁸ Be sober minded; be watchful. Your adversary the devil prowls around like a roaring lion, seeking someone to devour.

⁹ Resist him, firm in your faith, knowing that the same kinds of suffering are being experienced by your brotherhood throughout the world.

"When you change the way you look at things, the things you look at will change."

FOUR LAWS OF LIFE:

TO TALK TO AND HEAR FROM GOD

1. **HUMBLE THYSELF**
2. **PRAY**
3. **SEEK GOD'S FACE**
4. **TURN AWAY FROM THY WICKED WAYS**

Psalm 51:10-12 KJV

[10] Create in me a clean heart, O God; and renew a right spirit within me.

[11] Cast me not away from thy presence; And take not thy holy spirit from me.

[12] Restore unto me the joy of thy salvation; and uphold me with thy free spirit.

As I followed the four laws of life, I discovered that God can hear me and will never leave nor forsake me. Now, I'm falling deeper in prayers and meditation to seek him. Life can knock you down, but if we only master doing what's right, which is letting go and letting God lead the direction of our path we will be more beneficial and life will then be more fulfilling. Your past and present iniquities doesn't have to be your ending. There is life and purpose in your story.

Just when you believe everything is going well, the enemy is out hitting push ups waiting for you to excel!

God opened my eyes! He took away the habit of smoking and the addiction to alcohol and drugs.

He stripped away the desire to speak profanity out of my mouth and even the desire to fornicate.

On March 17, 2023, I married Jasmine Penn. Now introduced as Jasmine Arbuckle. God is amazing!

The devil tried to stop it all, but even through my iniquities I found favor in the Lord.

Proverbs 18:22 ESV
[22] He who finds a wife finds a good thing and obtains favor from the Lord.

GET BACK SATAN NOW

To whomever this may encourage, let us pray. Repent and repeat after me.

Father forgive me, I need you more than anything. I'm asking that you fill me up with the spirit of victory over all strongholds and darkness of this world. I plead the blood of Jesus over my life, over my thoughts and over my actions, that the spirit of the true living God may rest upon me and give me peace that surpasses all understanding, in Jesus name, Amen.

GET BACK SATAN, NOW!

If you would like to support and sow a seed you can send it via cash app
$GETBACKSATANNOW

LETS GET CONNECTED!

You can connect me at the link below
https://wisdom.app/getbacksatannow

Follow me on Facebook!
@getbacksatannow

Feel free to contact me:
(225)274-6928

www.ingramcontent.com/pod-product-compliance
Lightning Source LLC
Chambersburg PA
CBHW020432010526
44118CB00010B/543